# Bold Moves

## A Dancer's Journey

by

Barbara Rudow

Bold Moves: A Dancer's Journey
COPYRIGHT 2007
by Barbara Rudow

All rights reserved. Printed in the United States of America. No part of this book may be used or reproduced in any matter whatsoever without written permission, except in the case of brief quotations embodied in critical articles and reviews. For information about Scobre...

Scobre Press Corporation
2255 Calle Clara
La Jolla, CA 92037

Scobre Press books may be purchased for educational, business or sales promotional use. First Scobre edition published 2007.

Edited by Charlotte Graeber
Cover Art & Layout by Michael Lynch
Content Editing & Research by Katherine Shafer

ISBN # 1-933423-95-1

**TOUCHDOWN EDITION**
This story is based on the real life of Carolyn Lamour, although some names, quotes, and details of events have been altered.

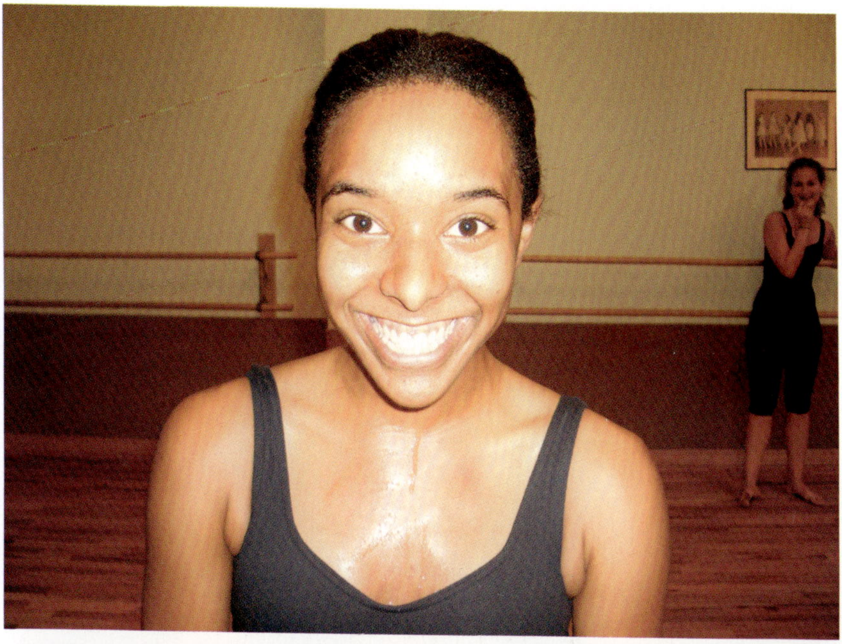

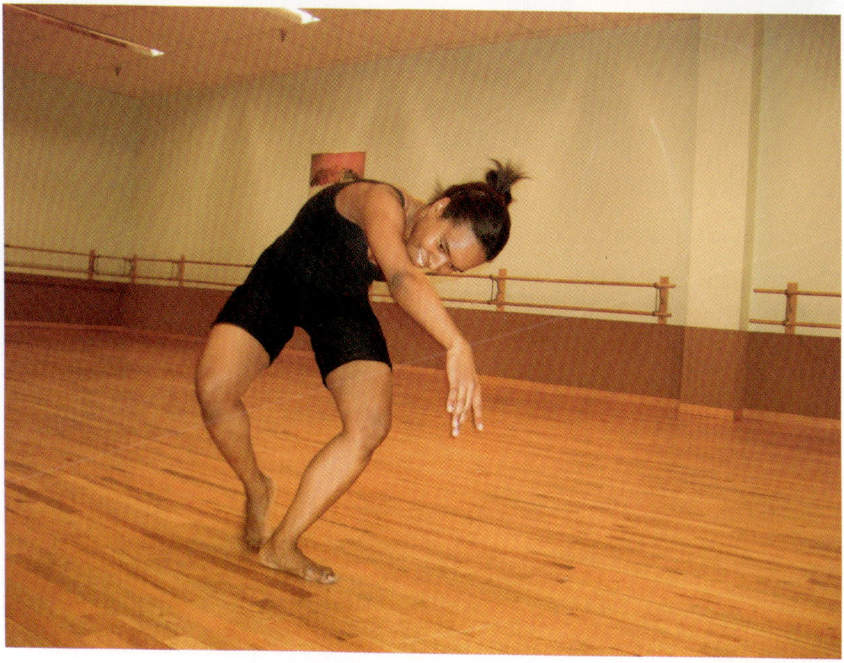

# Chapter One

## Magic Slippers

Dance is defined as the rhythmic movement of one's body in a pattern, often to the accompaniment of music. For those who love it, though, dance is so much more than that. Accurately defining dance with words is nearly impossible. That's because there is no exact science to it—no specific set of rules to apply and no unit of measurement available to analyze its principles. There is only the heart and soul of a dancer.

Dance is an art form. It's a physical expression of deep thoughts and feelings. When performed well, the movements of a dancer's body are as emotional as they are physical. Great dancers often talk about *feeling* the music inside of them as they create movements that belong to the music. When executed with this type of passion, dance is one of the most beautiful things in the world.

From the time she could walk, Carolyn Lamour was drawn to this beauty. The beat of an imaginary drum pounded within her, and the echo of every song she'd ever heard reverberated in her head. The music of her soul played from sunup till sundown—and she couldn't turn it off. Wherever she went, and whatever she did, the beat went on. Her desire to take ownership of the beat and to express herself through dance overwhelmed her.

At just three years old, Carolyn found an outlet for her passion. Each night after dinner, she would sneak into her 17-year-old cousin Patricia's room a few minutes before the teenager's ballet lesson. It was in that room, under their grandparents' roof, where Carolyn witnessed something that changed her world permanently.

In front of a full-length mirror, with music blasting in the background, Patricia would perform a beautiful ceremony. First, she would put on a beautiful, sparkly leotard that made her look like Cinderella. Next, she would put her hair up in an elegant bun and secure it with a matching pink ribbon. Finally, she'd slip into an incredible pair of dainty, pink lace-up slippers. In Carolyn's eyes, the slippers were magical—instantly transforming her cousin into a ballerina.

Once she put the magic slippers on, Patricia would glide across the wood floor with grace and ease. The world seemed to stand still in these moments. Carolyn would climb onto Patricia's bed and stare at her in awe. Nothing else existed… There was only Patricia, those slippers and the movements she seemed to perform so naturally. From the first time Carolyn witnessed the beauty of this dance, she knew that one day, she, too, would be a dancer.

By the time she was five years old Carolyn began dancing all the time, and she quickly developed her natural talent. Before long, she came to realize that dance was a part of her soul, pushing her forward as if it had a life of its own. Her passion was like a runaway train; there was no stopping it.

Carolyn is similar to many other great dancers, those who were never formally introduced to dance, but from a young age simply felt like they *had* to dance. For these natural-born dancers, moving to the beat was something they did simply because it felt right. This is the way superstar Jennifer Lopez describes her early passion for dance. She says, "…From the time I was very little, it was just something I would do all the time... It wasn't something that was fake or contrived."

Jennifer Lopez, also known as J-Lo, is a world-renowned

entertainer with a career rooted in dance. Wherever she performs, people are compelled to watch her, amazed that the human body can be so graceful, dynamic and alluring at the same time. J-Lo makes dancing look like the most natural thing in the world—because for her, it is. The movements of her body are in perfect rhythm with the music, and the results are beautiful.

Carolyn admires J-Lo for the way her popularity has helped to energize the dance world. Her versatile career as an entertainer is unmatched, with huge successes as an actress, dancer *and* singer. J-Lo has not only danced in her many music videos, but also in major films such as *Selena* and *Shall We Dance*. In 2007, she diversified her career even further, becoming the executive producer of the MTV reality show *Dance Life*. This show depicts the real-life trials and tribulations of dancers trying to make it as professionals in Hollywood—a place where competition is high. J-Lo says, "These dancers have dedicated their lives to this, and honestly, the glory is not always there. It's something they do only out of love."

As J-Lo alludes to above, the life of a dancer can be very hard. Carolyn understands this better than anyone. As a competitive dancer, she knows all about the long, hard hours of training, the intensity of auditions and the frustration you feel when you are not selected. After years of dancing, Carolyn is well aware of the hard road ahead of her. Professional dancing jobs are few and far between, so the pay is erratic. For every dancer that makes a living through her art form, hundreds of others are forced to quit after years of floundering from job to job. To succeed as a dancer, you have to love it *and* be willing to stick with it.

J-Lo stuck with a career that seemed to be going nowhere

for almost 20 years. She could have easily become discouraged and quit before she became the megastar she is today. Aside from a few paying jobs here and there, her career didn't really take off until about 10 years ago.

On her MTV show, she is often seen auditioning dancers, a process she remembers well. J-Lo got her first break at age 21 when she was cast as a "Fly Girl," dancing at the beginning and end of each episode of the 1990's TV comedy *In Living Color*. This job didn't pay much, and certainly didn't offer any guarantees of career longevity. Through hard work and dedication, though, J-Lo made her own breaks.

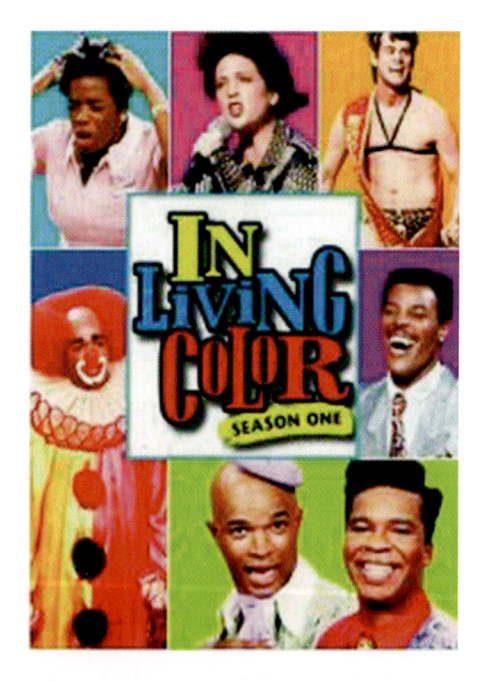

**In addition to twenty-one year old J-Lo, *In Living Color* introduced America to Jim Carrey, Damon Wayans and Jamie Foxx, all of whom went on to successful careers in entertainment.**

Born in 1989, Carolyn has never even seen the show *In Living Color*. Although she doesn't have much time available to watch TV at all, she *has* seen a few episodes of some more recent dance shows. Shows like *Dancing with the Stars* and *So You Think You Can Dance* have brought the dance world to center stage. In 2006, professional football player Emmitt Smith did for ballroom dancing what Mikhail Baryshnikov once did for ballet. When Emmitt Smith, the NFL's all-time rushing leader, won *Dancing with the Stars*, he made the world see that it was cool for men to dance, too.

It's interesting to note that many of the dancing and singing stars we see today got their starts on television shows as well. Britney Spears took dance and gymnastics lessons from a young age and performed in many local dance reviews. In 1993, she caught a break and began appearing on *The Mickey Mouse Club* show. That same TV show introduced a few other budding young stars: Justin Timberlake and Christina Aguilera both appeared onstage with Britney. All three of these singers have gone on to be huge stars. They all began their careers as teenage dancers who could sing. Ironically, each of them is now known for being a singer who can dance.

Although she is an accomplished dancer herself, Carolyn has never been on TV. Her career path has consisted mostly of competitive dancing in more traditional forms, such as ballet. Ballet is the art form which kick-started the career of another famous dancer: Madonna. The "Material Girl" started out as a ballerina, attending the University of Michigan on a dance scholarship. A few years later, she moved to New York with the hope of becoming a professional ballet dancer on Broadway. Although she didn't stick with ballet, Madonna was discovered in a New York club, while she was singing and dancing with the band Emmy. The rest is history.

Carolyn hopes to have her own dance success story one day. For now, she continues her ascension as one of the top young dancers in America. What does the future hold for Carolyn? The answers are linked to her past.

**Summer 1997: Carolyn and her family spend a day at the beach in Haiti.**

# Chapter Two

## From America to Haiti—and Back Again

Carolyn grew up in the Republic of Haiti, a rugged, beautiful country occupying the western third of the Caribbean island of Hispaniola. Sitting between the islands of Cuba to the west and Puerto Rico to the east, Hispaniola boasts tropical weather, incredible beaches and a rich variety of cultural experiences.

Most Haitians speak Haitian Creole, which is a cross between French and several traditional West African languages.

The languages mixed because Haitians are of African descent—yet Haiti was a French colony until it declared independence in 1804. A major religion in Haiti is Voodoo, a faith that has often been misunderstood throughout history. Only recently has it been practiced completely out in the open in Haiti.

In addition to the beautiful beaches and interesting culture, Haiti is famous for The Citadelle, an amazing palace built on a summit 900 meters high. This enormous architectural and engineering feat is often referred to as the Eighth Wonder of the World.

Today, however, the beautiful aspects of Carolyn's homeland are overshadowed by the many political problems that currently make Haiti an extremely violent place. Haiti is plagued by a corrupt government, gang-ridden streets, major drug trafficking, illiteracy and extreme poverty. The streets of Haiti are filled with danger and unpredictability. One of the saddest things going on in Haiti today has to do with its innocent children.

**A group of Haitian children on their way to school.**

Because 80 percent of the population lives in poverty, many children are not able to attend school. For those lucky enough to be students, there are few books and supplies. Still, you won't hear them complain. Many of their young friends and family members face a fate much worse than underfunded schools. Thousands of Haitian children are forced to skip their childhood altogether and work as household servants known as "restavecs." There are currently 170,000 child-servants on the island of Haiti. They have no opportunity to leave, and are often abused and mistreated.

Worst of all for Haitian children is the radicals' newest ploy: kidnapping children in an attempt to destabilize the government. Children are taken from their homes, off school buses and even from school itself. Some of the children are returned when a ransom is paid, but many of them are tortured and murdered.

This is not the Haiti that Carolyn Lamour remembers. Although Carolyn was born in Washington, D.C., her parents moved her back to Haiti when she was just eight months old. This is the country her family had lived in for generations, so it was natural for her parents to want Carolyn and her sister to grow up there.

A few years earlier, before Carolyn's birth, her parents had left Haiti and moved to the United States to attend school. They both dreamed of becoming doctors in America and then returning to Haiti to help the people there. To do that, though, they were required to spend very long hours at the hospital. The Lamours didn't want their children growing up with babysitters, so they headed back to Haiti where they entrusted Carolyn and her older sister, Isabel, to their grandparents. They all lived together in the capital city of Port-au-Prince.

It was a very difficult decision, but seemed like the only

logical choice. The plan was for the girls to live with their grand parents until Mr. and Mrs. Lamour completed their medical training. At that time, the family would reunite in Haiti. The flight to Haiti from Florida is only about 90 minutes, so Carolyn's parents were able to visit regularly. Still, the situation was less than ideal.

The Haitian home Carolyn grew up in was packed with people. Her grandparents' house was bursting at the seams: There was Carolyn, her sister, an aunt, an uncle, seven cousins and lots of chickens to help feed the large group. Carolyn remembers the house as a love-filled place where she would play with her sister and cousins in the tropical sun. She also remembers it as the place where she discovered dance—listening to Haitian music and watching her cousin Patricia in her ballet slippers each night.

**Carolyn's grandparents home in Haiti.**

Carolyn's and Isabel's days often revolved around something we take for granted in America: electricity. During the day the neighborhood kids would be outside playing… until they heard the

11

low hum of electricity. A distant noise grew like rolling thunder as the city turned on, one light at a time. Electricity was only available for a limited number of hours each day, so Carolyn learned to appreciate it. Even today in her home in America, you'll rarely see her absentmindedly leave a light on.

Carolyn lived in Haiti until 1994, leaving just after her fifth birthday. She knew no other life and was blissfully unaware of the changes that would soon make Haiti a dangerous place to live. By this time, Haiti was falling into total chaos. The people struggled to survive amid attempted military takeovers and extreme poverty. These political struggles left thousands dead. People fled the country in droves, desperate for a better life somewhere else.

Carolyn's family was no exception. Her parents knew that Haiti was no longer safe for their children, so they decided to change their plans and bring Isabel and Carolyn back to live in America. By this time Carolyn also had a little brother, Jean-Paul. It was decided that he would remain with his grandparents until he was old enough to attend school. Like his sisters, they didn't want Jean-Paul to spend his childhood with babysitters. Separating the family again was a painful decision for everyone.

Carolyn tired to understand, but she was too young to fully grasp the situation. She loved Haiti and wanted her parents to live there so they could all be together. Leaving her grandparents, her cousins and her home was terribly hard. Although she was happy to be with her parents, Carolyn cried through the entire flight to the United States.

When Carolyn got to America, she lived in Washington, D.C.—the city she was born in, but knew little about. Within a year her parents decided to move to Lake Worth, Florida—to be closer to their family in Haiti and to live in the warm tropical weather they'd been accustomed to their entire lives. Plus, Carolyn's father, Jean-Michael, loves to garden so they bought property where they could grow star fruit, mangos, plantains and sugarcane. They tried to create an environment that was reminiscent of their life in Haiti.

**The island nation of Haiti is very close to Florida.**

    Florida was *not* Haiti, though, and Carolyn went through some difficult adjustments. The biggest hurdle she faced was that she didn't speak English—just French and Creole. At home, her parents made the girls speak only English so they would learn the language quickly. Carolyn recalls lying in bed at night, speaking Creole with Isabel as they reminisced about Haiti.
    Everything seemed hard for Carolyn when she first arrived at school. After all, she couldn't communicate with her teachers or

any of the other kids. The work seemed impossible. Once she mastered English, though, things got easier. She made friends and found that she had a strong aptitude as a student. Carolyn's mother, Lydie, still laughs about the time Carolyn wrote a note to her teachers asking them for *more* homework.

The extra time Carolyn had on her hands didn't last long. After a conversation with her mom about after-school activities, she was immediately enrolled in ballet class. At first, Carolyn was very excited about the class. "I'm going to dance just like Patricia," she told her mother. Visions of her cousin and those magic slippers filled her head. But her class wasn't the glamorous experience she imagined it to be. Ballet requires hard, repetitive work—especially early on in one's training. Carolyn just wanted to *dance*!

Ballet training begins by learning all the different positions of the hands and feet. A young ballet dancer won't actually dance until she has mastered all the movements—one at a time. The process takes a lot of patience.

The "first position" of the feet is with the heels touching and the toes pointed out to the sides. The "second position" also has the toes pointed outward, but now the heels are apart, aligned under the shoulders. The "third position" is when one foot is crossed to the middle of the other foot, also with the toes pointed outward. From there one must learn more advanced positions, where the toes are pointed outward while the feet are both crossed and separated.

These positions are the stepping stones to learning ballet. For a young girl who just wanted to magically glide across the floor, they seemed stupid and boring. So, after a few frustrating months, five-year-old Carolyn decided that ballet wasn't for her. She threw away her Pooh Bear leotard as well as her dreams of becoming a dancer.

At home, though, she never stopped dancing. Sure, her form was off, and her skills were raw, but she truly *felt* the music and could move gracefully to any beat. She danced in front of her mirror every day, pretending to be a famous ballerina. Just as J-Lo did when she was young, Carolyn got her first stage experience by putting on dance performances for anyone willing to watch. That meant family, friends, neighbors and even her stuffed animals.

Carolyn eventually found her way back to formal dance classes three years later, when she was eight. By this time, she was beginning to understand that becoming a great dancer didn't happen overnight. Dance deserved another chance—so she enrolled in ballet and tap at a studio called That's Dancing and quickly discovered her true calling.

This time around, she breezed through the foot positions and moved onto the barre, which is a ballet term for a handrail that the dancer holds onto while executing various dance steps. It is designed to help dancers maintain proper body-position. Carolyn thought the barre exercises were just as tedious as learning the beginning foot positions. Still, she understood that the barre was an important tool that would take her one step closer to her dream—to dance as beautifully as her cousin in those magic slippers.

**A ballerina stretches while holding onto the barre.**

Like the foot positions, there is a specific order to the barre. The first move Carolyn had to master was the plié, which is French for "bent." This is a move where the knees are bent over the toes, deep enough so that the thighs are parallel to the floor. This is a critical move in ballet. Once mastered, a dancer can move on to more advanced moves like the tendu, the rond de jambe and the frappé.

Although Carolyn felt very awkward and uncoordinated at the beginning, once she started learning the moves, dancing became really fun. Carolyn found herself dancing *everywhere*: down the halls, through the kitchen, and even among the clothes racks at the mall.

Perhaps just as important as the dancing itself, Carolyn had found a place she belonged. That's Dancing is owned by two sisters, Andrea LaMaina and Michele Walsh. They were more than just talented instructors; they were friends. Miss Andrea, as Carolyn calls her, became Carolyn's primary instructor and choreographer. Carolyn credits her as being her inspiration. The studio became her home away from home; the dancers and instructors were like a second family. This was important for a girl from Haiti, struggling to find her identity in America.

As she improved, her passion for dance grew. Within a year, dance was far and away the biggest thing in Carolyn's life. Three years after leaving Haiti, she was living her dream—and it seemed as if nothing could stop her.

# Chapter Three

## Keep Dancing

From the time she was born, Carolyn battled asthma, which is a medical condition that causes inflammation of the airways. The muscles surrounding the tubes that carry air into the lungs go into spasm, causing fluid to build up in the lungs. This makes breathing difficult and painful. Carolyn controlled her asthma as much as possible by using a daily medicine inhaler. This allowed her to dance without too much interference.

Having asthma is a major hardship for any athlete to endure. Plus, asthma can cause damage to the lungs. Because of this, Carolyn had x-rays taken regularly to make sure that her lungs were healthy. She had them taken at her father's clinic. On one occasion, while looking over Carolyn's pictures, as her father called them, he was unusually quiet. He studied the x-ray carefully and produced a deep sigh. Although he was relieved to see that Carolyn's lungs were fine, he was disturbed by what else he saw: Carolyn's thoracic spine (upper back) was significantly curved. It appeared that Carolyn had a condition known as scoliosis.

Scoliosis is a curvature of the spine that can lead to physical deformities, pain and medical complications. Scoliosis causes the spine to twist and the vertebrae (the bones that make up the spine) to rotate. That movement causes the rib cage to be displaced, forming a rib hump. If you look at the back of a person with scoliosis, you can see a hump on one side of the spine. Two out of every 1,000 people have scoliosis. It is more common in women than in men. For most people, the curve is so slight that treatment is not required. Unless the degree of curve goes over 25 degrees, it's not really a problem.

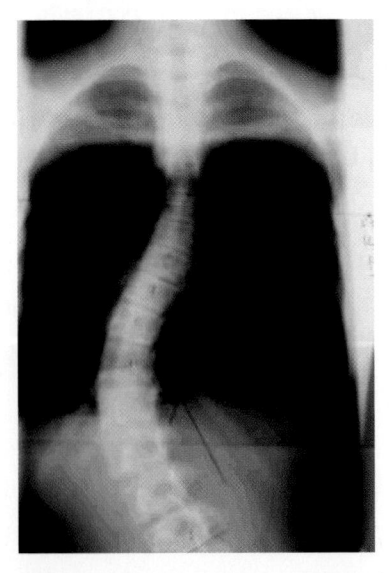

**The x-ray above shows the curved spine of a person who suffers from severe scoliosis.**

Carolyn was immediately sent to a specialist to determine if she were lucky enough to fall into the "under 25 degrees" category. She sat on the hospital cot in her blue gown, waiting for the orthopedic doctor to come back with her x-rays. Because she couldn't *see* her spine, it was hard to comprehend how her condition might be affecting her. Her mother, an experienced physician, sat beside her and tried to explain everything. Carolyn found it hard to listen. Powerful emotions ran through her as she waited: frustration, confusion and fear. She was completely overwhelmed. After all, she was just 10 years old. Life was supposed to be simple and fun.

"I just want to go home," she moaned, as her mother tried to comfort her.

After what seemed like an eternity, the doctor came back. He confirmed that Carolyn did have scoliosis, and unfortunately, it was pretty severe. While he explained everything, he put her x-rays up on the viewing machine. Carolyn will never forget seeing her x-ray alongside a "normal" spine x-ray. The difference between the two pictures was scary. Carolyn could clearly see that her spine was crooked. This explained the back pain that she often felt. After seeing her x-ray, everything started to make sense.

Although Carolyn could see the problem, she still was not quite sure what it meant. The doctor mentioned that Carolyn's curve was already at 30 degrees. He went on to say that scoliosis often gets worse as a person grows, so this was a very significant curve for a 10-year-old. It was clear that Carolyn's condition was going to seriously limit her physical activities—mainly, her dancing.

There are several different opinions on how to treat scoliosis. Some specialists believe that if you try to stop the spine from twisting right away, you can control the degree of the curve and prevent it from getting much worse. Because Carolyn was so young and had a desire to dance, her parents decided to try this.

Carolyn started out by wearing the Charleston brace, otherwise known as the "nighttime" brace. The brace is made of hard plastic and is molded to fit the child. The hope is that while the brace is on, the curvature slows down. The nice thing about this brace is that it allows the child to move freely during the day, because it is only worn at night. Carolyn cringes when she recalls the brace and how uncomfortable it was to sleep in.

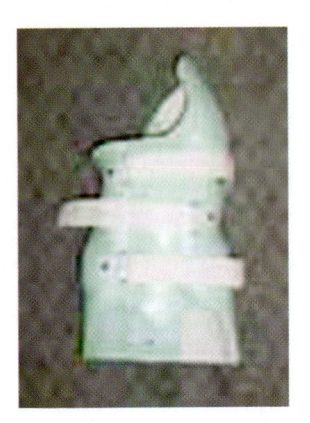

Still, that brace wasn't too traumatic for her. The key was that she didn't have to wear it in public. Carolyn slept in it every night and continued to dance every day. Although her back definitely caused her pain during this time, she hardly ever complained. In fact, she even added additional dance classes to her schedule, hoping to make her back stronger. Because ballet works the body symmetrically, it can help to improve balance and coordination, which for Carolyn had always been a bit off due to her scoliosis. She also started doing back exercises daily, to help strengthen the muscles supporting her spine.

Despite the brace and all of her exercises, the curve continued to worsen during the next few years. By the time she began middle school, the curve had become very apparent. Carolyn's curve was primarily in her thoracic spine, so her right shoulder was noticeably higher than the left. She found herself having to compensate for that by adjusting her balance constantly. That was extremely difficult in ballet, because perfect alignment is critical. The fact that Carolyn can dance as well as she does—with severe scoliosis—is nothing short of miraculous.

As a 12-year-old, Carolyn couldn't help being embarrassed by her lopsided appearance. There were some nights when she cried herself to sleep over it. More often than not, though, she displayed an uncommon strength that pushed her forward, despite her handicap. Instead of letting her appearance bother her, she focused all of her attention on dance, and on finding a way to make her crooked body balanced and straight. As her condition worsened, Carolyn had to work twice as hard, fighting against the odds to be the graceful ballerina she knew she could be.

That same year, in sixth grade, Carolyn entered her first group competition with That's Dancing. In this competition, 25 dancers performed together. Carolyn recalls being backstage, joking around with her friends, not fully understanding what it meant to compete. When Carolyn stepped out on the stage, though, she felt her nerves tighten. After a few scared moments, she looked around at the other dancers and relaxed a bit. She danced well, although she didn't think it was her best performance. Her team took third place in the competition.

Carolyn's dance instructor, Andrea, saw that first competition completely differently. She recalls watching Carolyn's performance and noticing immediately that there was something special about her. In short, she lit up the stage. She was not only talented, but she was also tough—two qualities you need to make it in the dance world.

**Carolyn and Miss Andrea.**

"Throughout all of our years together," Andrea says, "Carolyn never used her scoliosis as an excuse." In fact, most of the dancers at the studio didn't even know Carolyn had scoliosis, even though it made dancing painful and 10 times as challenging for her.

Despite her circumstances, Carolyn was having fun. She loved performing, so it was no surprise that she decided to go to the next level, which meant performing in solo competitions. To really stand out when competing alone she would have to attempt more difficult steps. This would require more of her body. Because Carolyn wanted to continue her group competitions, she had to train for both. This meant long hours at the studio, sometimes up to eight per day. In addition to dance training, she was doing everything the doctors asked of her, but her scoliosis wasn't responding.

**Working hard at the studio.**

In the summer after sixth grade, Carolyn found herself once again sitting in the doctor's office, waiting for x-rays. This time she knew what the doctor was going to say before he spoke. After all, she could feel her condition worsening. No x-rays were needed for her to come to this realization. The intense pain in her back spoke louder and more clearly than any doctor could.

Shortly after watching the doctor review the x-ray, her suspicions were confirmed. Not only had her thoracic curve increased, but she also now had a curve in her lumbar spine (her lower back). The next words out of the doctor's mouth nearly crushed Carolyn's spirit. "I'm sorry," he said, "but from this point forward, you're going to have to wear a full-time body brace."

Carolyn barely heard anything the doctor said after that. The room seemed to spin and the sounds of the hospital were muted. She tried to hold back tears as she thought about what this would mean for her upcoming solo debut and the rest of her life beyond that. The future seemed dark and uncertain.

The new brace was an underarm brace that was much more cumbersome than her night brace. This brace was also molded out of plastic, but was specifically designed to help lift one shoulder. There was no way to hide it either. Loose clothing could disguise some of it, but anyone with two eyes could see that there was something odd about Carolyn's posture. Unfortunately, the brace had to be worn for 23 hours a day. That meant that she had to wear it *everywhere*—to school, social events and, as she got older, even on dates. The only time she was allowed to take the brace off was when she was showering.

Although she had no choice but to wear the brace, she did ask the doctors if she could make one exception: She wanted permission to take the brace off when she danced. She had tried dancing with the brace on, but her movements were so restricted that she couldn't perform well.

There is no documented research that proves a back brace

will stop the spine from continuing to move. Without guaranteed results, the doctors decided that Carolyn's request to remove the brace while dancing was acceptable—for the time being.

In the meantime, Carolyn tried very hard not to let the brace upset her life. That was not always easy. When she returned to school for seventh grade, there was no place to hide. She was at a new school, where the kids didn't know about her scoliosis. Most of her classmates were nice, although their curious stares sometimes hurt as much as the occasional mean comment. Nothing was worse than when some jerk would tap her on her "plastic" back as he walked by her in the hallways. What hurt the most, though, was that Carolyn felt as if she were different.

Blocking out the *physical* pain proved to be much easier for her. Although the brace was pushing her spine in directions it didn't want to go, all day, every day, Carolyn persevered. Deep within herself she found the strength to ignore the pain, and to close her eyes to the disfigurement she saw in the mirror. During this trying time, Carolyn did the only thing she could—she kept dancing.

# Chapter 4

## Disco Ball

During the spring of seventh grade, Carolyn competed in her first solo competition. She had auditioned for the competition dance company Fusion Force and made it easily. A competition dance team is called a "company" and is made up of the best dancers at a particular studio. That's Dancing has about 700 dancers of varying levels, but only about 20 make it into the dance company.

Carolyn's instructors were confident that she would be a great solo performer. They felt that her natural talent and dynamic personality could captivate any audience. Although Carolyn had yet to win a major competition, she was respected by her peers in the dance company. They even gave her the nickname "Carolyn the Great."

**Carolyn, (bottom right) poses for a photo with her dance group while backstage at a recital.**

    Dance competitions are grueling and can unnerve even the most experienced dancers. This competition, which took place in Fort Lauderdale, Florida, was no exception. Unlike group competitions, where the girls prepare together backstage, dancers wait alone in their respective dressing rooms for solo competitions.

    While in her dressing room, Carolyn took off her back brace to stretch. Next, she put on her costume. It was a beautiful red velvet leotard with a flowing skirt that twirled above her knees. She would be dancing to the song "Love in Any Language," which had been choreographed for her by Andrea. Carolyn wanted to make her mentor proud, but she was so nervous that she could barely pull up her long, red gloves.

The lyrical dance competition, which is a combination of ballet and jazz, requires an array of skills. The actual techniques displayed here are very traditional, but the dance is more fluid, almost like it's telling a story. Dancers are judged on their ability to express and interpret the lyrics through the choreography. The lyrics are the inspiration for the movement, but it's up to the dancer to make the performance come alive. Carolyn's incredible talent, combined with her commanding presence on the stage, made this a natural art form for her. She had a remarkable way of bringing every dance move to life.

Backstage, Carolyn wasn't thinking about any of that. Instead, she was nervously chewing on her fingernails—trying hard not to think about the packed auditorium or the fact that she would soon be all alone in front of the judges. Not unlike the TV show *American Idol*, the judges sit in the front row, ready to dissect every move. It is definitely a nerve-wracking experience for first-time solo competitors.

Like all the dancers, Carolyn sprayed glitter on her body to make her shimmer as she danced. Carolyn's nerves distracted her, though, and without realizing what she was doing, she continued to apply the glitter. It was as if she thought she could drown the butterflies in her stomach by covering them in sparkles. When it was finally her turn to perform, she put the glitter away and nervously made her way to center stage.

This particular dance starts with Carolyn on her knees, curled down into a ball, as she performs expressive arm movements. (Andrea later confessed that with all of the glitter she'd put on,

Carolyn looked like a disco ball!) From the curled position, the dance flows into a series of turns and steps. Finally, Carolyn performs her signature move, the arabesque.

**The arabesque.**

  The arabesque is a very difficult dance move. By choosing this move in her first solo competition, Carolyn made a confident statement. The arabesque is executed by standing on one leg, with the other leg extended behind the body. The upper back maintains an upright position. When done correctly, this is a beautiful move. Because of the curvature of her spine, it is extremely difficult for Carolyn. She practiced long and hard to overcome the imbalance caused by her scoliosis, and to make the arabesque look perfect.

  Her first performance was clearly a major success, but to the trained eye of Miss Andrea, Carolyn still had a ways to go. She received a High Silver from the judges (the fourth highest award behind Platinum, High Gold and Gold), but Andrea knew Carolyn was capable of performing better. Her prized student hadn't danced nearly as well as she did in the studio. She was simply too nervous to dance freely. Andrea had to find a way to help tame Carolyn's nerves or she would never live up to her coach's expectations.

Although Carolyn tried to remain calm, the next several competitions were just as shaky. Andrea would try to talk her through the pre-dance jitters, but Carolyn's nerves continued to sabotage her performances.

Finally, in an important competition the following season, almost a full year after Carolyn's first solo performance, Miss Andrea had seen enough. She went backstage to find Carolyn, who was waiting to perform "Rosemary's Granddaughter." This dance would require a move called "turn in second." This turn is done on the toes of one foot. Carolyn must balance on her toes while the other leg is out to the side, perpendicular to her outstretched leg. With her arms out to the side, she must plié, and then turn her head to the side, so that her body follows in a quick, rotational turn. This is a difficult move for any dancer, but it's especially hard on Carolyn's crooked spine. Her body would never cooperate if she were tense. The move would look forced and awkward.

In a desperate attempt to help Carolyn break free of her nerves, Miss Andrea held Carolyn's hand… and threatened her! She looked her straight in the face, trying hard not to smile, and said, "I will cut your feet off if you don't dance like you do in the studio." There was a stunned silence from the other dancers who overheard this exchange.

After a strange moment, Carolyn began laughing so hard that she could barely contain herself. For some reason, this joke loosened her up—and from then on, Carolyn thought of it whenever she needed to shake her nerves.

By the time Carolyn was 15, she had become a regular on the dance circuit, winning many regional titles in west Florida. Aside from her success locally, she had yet to capture first place in a *national* competition. That became her new goal. Her first step in achieving that goal was to add more technical dance classes to her demanding schedule. She didn't mind the extra work—in fact, she loved it! Carolyn had become addicted to performing and couldn't imagine life without it. That's why her next doctor's appointment was so disturbing.

After another x-ray and a few minutes in the doctor's office, Carolyn was told that once again, her spine had worsened. The doctor told her to *consider* surgery as an option. Carolyn tried not to panic, but just the mention of surgery scared her. Surgery is usually done if there is unbearable back pain, decreased lung function or serious deformity as a result of the scoliosis. Surgery to correct scoliosis involves inserting a metal rod along the length of the spine to hold the body in an upright position—permanently.

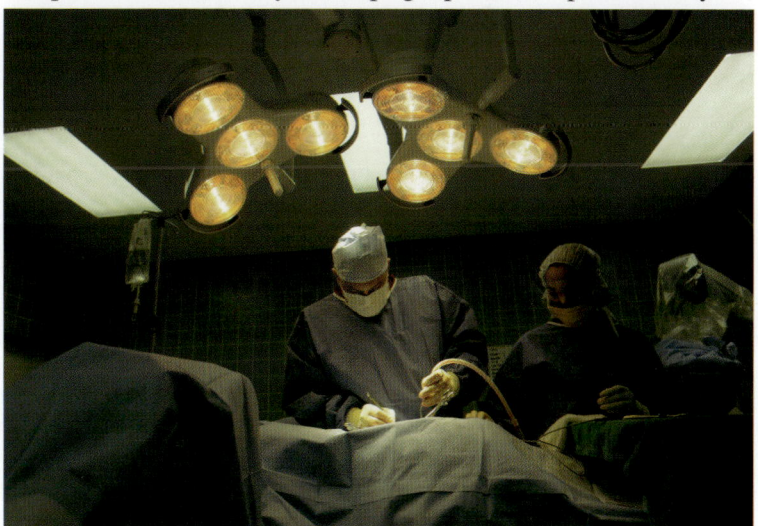

Carolyn will do whatever she can to avoid having life-altering back surgery.

In addition, bone grafts (grafting means taking bone from one area of the body and using it somewhere else) are added to the curved area to fuse it in the correct position. The bone needed for this is usually taken from the pelvis. Surgeons prefer to do this surgery before the problem becomes too severe because the results are better. As with any surgery, there are risks—such as movement of the rods in the back, infection, or nerve damage. Plus, there is a chance that the grafts don't take.

Although three months after surgery there are usually no restrictions on the patient's movements, Carolyn knew that surgery would end her dance career. The doctor made that clear. The surgery would stop her back from worsening, but it would limit her flexibility for the rest of her life. Carolyn and her parents discussed her options. They decided that although she may need the surgery in the future, for now she wasn't ready to give up dancing.

Instead, Carolyn decided to try *another* brace: the Copes brace. This brace has holes in the chest area with air vectors that adjust the pressure. This allowed Carolyn to adjust the brace as the curvature of her spine changed. She wasn't going to let scoliosis win—one way or another, she was going to keep dancing.

To further stall the curvature of her spine, Carolyn added additional back and abdominal exercises. She also stretched for over an hour each day, faithfully balancing on her exercise ball and repeatedly doing back raises to strengthen her lower back. She worked her abdominals hard and lifted weights to strengthen her upper back. She wore her brace every moment of every day, except when she danced. Through all of this, she never complained, she never felt sorry for herself, and most importantly, she never gave up.

**Because of her back issues, Carolyn has to stretch and stretch and stretch...**

Most times, as a way to deal with the painful brace, Carolyn would make light of it. She'd tell unsuspecting people about how she had been working on a new abdominal routine that gave her rock-hard abs. Then she told them to tap her stomach and laughed at their expressions when they felt the hard plastic brace.

Carolyn continued to excel in dance, but her schedule became so demanding that she decided to be home schooled during her sophomore year. This would allow her to keep up with her studies while also giving her more time for physical therapy and dance. This was a sacrifice she needed to make if she wanted to stay healthy and be a competitive dancer. For better or worse, sacrificing for dance was something Carolyn had gotten used to over the years.

# Chapter Five

## Kidnapped

    Before the start of Carolyn's sophomore year, the Lamour family decided to make another trip to beautiful Haiti. By this time, Carolyn's brother, Jean-Paul, had returned to Florida to live with his family. Still, the Lamours visited Haiti every chance they got. Carolyn's parents knew that the summer of 2004 might be the last time they would go there for a while. The violence and political climate were terrible, and it was becoming unsafe to travel there.

    When she first arrived, Carolyn tried to pretend that Haiti had not changed. Her early memories were all centered on her grandparents and cousins. These memories remained unbroken. From the time she turned down the gravel road and glanced at the water tank perched on the roof of her grandparents' home in Port-au-Prince, it was as if she had stepped back in time. There was laughter, singing and the usual goofing around.

However, now that Carolyn was older, she was forced to see Haiti with a new set of eyes. The merchants walking the streets with baskets of goods balanced on their heads were no longer just a convenient way to shop—they were poor people trying to survive. The children who flanked their car to wash the windshield were no longer amusing—they were hungry, tired and stricken by poverty. Carolyn found out that her grandfather, a Haitian attorney, didn't actually go on "vacation" a few years earlier, but was hiding out from officials who wanted him dead because they did not like the way one of his cases had gone in court. Being back in Haiti as a teenager was upsetting. Carolyn's memories took on new shapes and formed an unwelcoming reality.

The violence in Haiti had gotten much worse. Most schools were closing because of safety concerns for the children. Whenever they left home they had to travel in groups to avoid kidnappers. The Haiti of her past was gone. In light of this, many Haitians were desperately attempting to flee. Leaving Haiti is difficult for most people, because unlike Carolyn and her family, they aren't U.S. citizens. It is difficult to get safe, legal means of entry into the United States. Many Haitians flee their homeland in unsafe, rickety boats, hoping for asylum (protection from another government that is granted to refugees) wherever they land. They are so scared of the violence, or so broken by the poverty, that they will do anything to seek a new life —even risk death on the open ocean.

Less than two years after their last visit to Haiti, on Christmas Eve of 2005, the Lamours became victims of the violence they had been trying to escape. Carolyn's cousin Olivier was kidnapped. He was like a brother to her, and needless to say, she and her family were terrified.

Olivier and a friend had gone to the local pizza parlor to get food for the group. He and his friend were excitedly talking and didn't notice a dark van that pulled up alongside them. By the time they realized what was happening, it was too late. Three men jumped out with guns and forced them into the van. They thought about trying to run, but they were outnumbered and feared being shot. One minute they were two fun-loving teenagers on their way home to their families; the next moment they were terrified victims of senseless violence.

For the Lamours, that Christmas will always be associated with fear and sadness. When Christmas morning dawned, beautifully wrapped presents with cheerful bows tied around them sat beneath the tree. But there was no joy. Carolyn curled up on the couch with her sister and tearfully recalled all the fun times they'd had with Olivier in Haiti. As they sat by the phone and waited for news, they prayed that he and his friend would not be harmed.

The family received a ransom letter two days later. The

amount requested was obscenely high and Olivier's parents could not pay it. One of Carolyn's relatives negotiated with the kidnappers to get the ransom reduced, but it was still out of reach. Family members and friends chipped in, but they still did not have enough money.

They paid what they had and were desperately trying to decide what to do next when they got a lucky break. Six days after the kidnapping, one of the kidnappers took pity on Olivier and his friend and decided to release them. While the other kidnappers were asleep, he dropped the kids off in a remote area about an hour from Port-au-Prince. It was the middle of the night and they had to walk in the shadows, for fear of being kidnapped again. The following morning, Olivier and his friend both made it safely back. They were lucky. Still, their lives, and the lives of their families, would never be the same.

Olivier has since sought political asylum in Canada. He may be safe now, but many of Carolyn's family members and friends still face that kind of terror in Haiti every day.

The kidnapping was horrifying for Carolyn. It saddened her that the home of her childhood was gone. She often wonders, "Will I ever go back to Haiti? Will I ever see my grandparents, cousins and friends again?"

These are powerful questions for Carolyn. The experiences and people that have made up her life are in jeopardy of solely existing as faded memories. Not being able to stay connected to her past is painful for Carolyn. As is the case with most great dancers, her life experiences often come to light in her expressive dance.

# Chapter Six

# Dancing Through Time

Dance can be found in some form in nearly every culture throughout history. Dance has been a major part of social and religious occasions. Magical and religious dances often asked the gods to provide rain, end famine or cure illness. The only constant in dance over time has been its ability to allow people to express their feelings with the earth and with each other.

In the Middle Ages, the infamous Dance of Death was performed daily by thousands in an attempt to ward off illness. A dancer, representing death, led the ritual procession of dancers. This dance was performed during the years of the Black Death, when the bubonic plague (a disease spread by rodents and fleas) made its way across Europe and Asia, killing almost one half of the population. The dance was considered both beautiful and grotesque. It was performed to express the feelings of people who were in the grasp of this deadly disease.

Dancing is represented in every ethnic group as well. Over time, things constantly evolve, but dancing definitely has a different style in different parts of the world. In Japan, dance is often formal and slow, unlike the lively Tango, which hails from South America.

Above, traditional Japanese dancers move gracefully and in perfect sync. Below, a couple dances the Tango in the streets of Rio de Janeiro, Brazil.

The Spaniards claim the Salsa and the red-hot Flamenco dance. The Irish are famous for the Clog dance and the Irish jig, from which tap dancing got its start.

**Two Spaniards (left) dance the Flamenco, while an Irish girl (right) performs a traditional jig.**

Native American dancers are known for their unique movements and ritual dances. They move to the beat of the drum and emphasize each movement of their feet and the posture of their heads.

A Native America chief performs a war dance.

     Probably the most famous individual dance of all time came from Europe: the Waltz. The Waltz became the rage in the 17$^{th}$ century because it represented freedom. Unlike traditional dances, which were performed the same by every dancer, the Waltz allowed dancers to sway across the floor in any direction they chose. The Waltz, like ballet, is still danced today.

     Ballet dancing has been around even longer than the Waltz. This type of dance started to pop up in the 16$^{th}$ century and was first performed in palaces and during feasts in Europe. Ballet became so popular that members of royalty would hire instructors to give them private lessons. By the 17$^{th}$ century, ballet had been elevated to an even higher stature, when it was performed in opera houses across Europe. In the 18th century, ballet became more focused on the spiritual world and on expressing emotions. This was when "pointe" work started, where dancers were actually up on the tips of their toes and seemed to magically glide across the stage.

It wasn't until the 20th century, however, that the most creative growth in ballet occurred. This was also the time when ballet became popular in the United States. People were experiencing new freedoms, and they expressed them through their dance. Modern dance took off, combining the traditional beauty of ballet with more daring movements—often shocking conservative viewers. Modern dance allowed traditional ballet dancers to be freer in their movements and more expressive in their interpretations of the music.

By the late 20th century, other types of dance started popping up. Michael Jackson and The Jackson Five introduced street dance. Break dancing was considered outrageous when it was first introduced, but it became wildly popular. Break dancing eventually evolved into what is known today as hip-hop dancing.

**Break dancing.**

Hip-hop dance has since taken on a life of its own—the movements are unorthodox, expressive and often go along with the beat and rhythm of the music. Unlike ballet and jazz, there is not a specific term for each move. Hip-hop dancing doesn't require formal training either, because of the free-form associated with the mostly improvised movements.

Good hip-hop dancers like Justin Timberlake, Janet Jackson and Usher make it look very easy. They have added to the popularity of this dance style by featuring it in music videos and on MTV. It has become so popular that now even traditional dance studios (like the one where Carolyn trains) are offering hip-hop classes. Even hip-hop is subject to change, though. We are already seeing it evolve as the music of our culture changes. Hip-hop used to be associated with fast, funky moves, but the new style of hip-hop has become slower and heavier.

These various styles may seem very different, but they are all used for the same purpose: to express oneself through dance. Most dancers today combine elements from all different dance styles. Hip-hop often incorporates jazz moves, and pop dancers often use techniques from many different styles, including elements of ballet, to interpret lyrics for their videos. The lyrical dance that Carolyn performs is no different.

When Carolyn steps on a stage, she is there not only to execute specific moves from many dance styles, but she is also there to interpret the music for the audience. She is expressive and passionate, bringing the song to life. Carolyn has a special gift in this area. She speaks to the audience through each movement. Her amazing grace and beauty, combined with her precise technique, have propelled Carolyn to the forefront of the dancing world.

By 2006, Carolyn had become the dancer to beat at major competitions. The year before, Carolyn had won her first Senior Solo competition, in addition to other titles. She was named the Regional Teen Miss Headliner and was selected an alternate on the U.S. Dance Team! Her career as a dancer had officially taken off. From this point forward, taking first place in regional competitions was expected.

The Headliners National Championship in 2006 was a chance for Carolyn to begin making a splash nationally. This competition offered Carolyn the chance to win her first *national* title, as well as a chance to represent the United States in the upcoming world competition.

Headliners is a dance organization that travels to different cities and offers many types of dance competitions. When Carolyn participated in the 2006 competition, it was held in Lancaster, Pennsylvania. This week-long competition had Carolyn performing in three separate categories, which is a typical schedule for a big competition. When dancing gets to this level, it takes a big commitment from the entire family because the competitions are so long. Carolyn's father usually stays home with her brother while her mom, although a busy physician, adjusts her work schedule around the seven days of events.

Carolyn's mother is more than just a devoted fan—she also makes all of her daughter's costumes. Andrea always has a definite vision in mind for the costumes, but she could never find exactly the right one. Over time, Carolyn's mother came to the rescue. Costumes are a critical part of every performance, so being able to make the perfect costume is a huge bonus.

In this competition, Carolyn was doing modern dance,

something she really enjoys. She was performing to the song "Blackbird." The problem is that this type of dance is harder on her body. Modern dance requires more contractions and more dance steps that force Carolyn to move from an upright position to dance steps that are done completely on the floor.

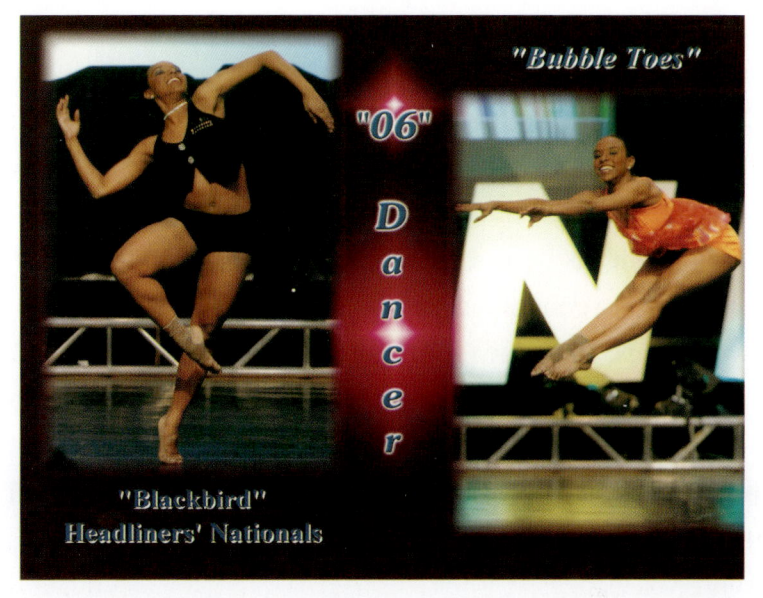

"06" Dancer

"Bubble Toes"

"Blackbird"
Headliners' Nationals

    The first move in this dance is a simple run across the stage. When Carolyn gets to the center, she stops and moves directly into a graceful leap. Those first moves are critical, as they are the first impression the judges get. At this competition, the stage was raised, so Carolyn didn't have to look eye-level at the judges. She liked this better—distancing herself from the judging process allowed her to focus more on the actual dance.

    The judges give numerical scores for each performance. During the performance, the judges speak softly into microphones, critiquing the dance. The dancers get to keep the tapes after the dance so they know how they were scored and what they might need to improve on.

Carolyn's first dance of the competition was critical. If she performed well enough, she would be chosen to represent the United States in the upcoming world competition in Germany. A spot on the U.S. Dance Team meant that she would be one of a select group of dancers, less than 20 in total, who would represent the United States at the International Dance Organization World Championships. Obviously, this would be a great honor.

As with any dance competition, you never know exactly what the judges are looking for. For example, if they don't think your costume fits the dance, you are marked off. If they don't think the song was a good choice for you, they mark you off. And then there's the performance itself: Did they like your choreography? Were you precise, yet graceful, in your movements? Did you leap high enough? Did the judges connect with you? Did you connect with the audience? Did you point each toe? Each judge is different, too. Even if you think you danced flawlessly, you might not do as well as you thought.

Carolyn's dance only lasted two minutes and 19 seconds, but it seemed like forever. She had a problem with her costume that she had to try to ignore during the entire dance. Her shorts were slipping down and she couldn't use her hands to pull them up. On each leap she prayed that they wouldn't fall! That would have been a disaster. Somehow, she was able to stay focused and block it out, focusing only on her dance.

After all the dancers had performed, they were called back onto the stage together. Carolyn recalls being more nervous standing there than she was through her entire dance. Her hands were sweaty and her heart raced as she stared into the blinding spotlight.

The judges called the dancers' names one at a time—then each of the judges held up a card with a number on it. That number represented what place the judge thought the dancer came in. Numbers one and two would be going to Germany. The others were eliminated, hoping (like Carolyn the year before) that they would get another chance the following year.

Because the judges pick the dancers individually, they do not usually all agree and vote for the same dancer. In this case, they did. Carolyn was selected as the number one dancer by every single judge. In a landslide, she had been placed on the United States Dance Team! She was definitely living up to the nickname "Carolyn the Great."

# Chapter Seven

## Sacrifice

After making her way onto the United States Dance Team, Carolyn felt like she was on top of the world. Her road to success had not been easy, though. When Carolyn started dancing at age eight, it was just a fun way to pass the time. Eventually, it became so much more than that—it became her life's passion. There are millions of people who love to dance. Many of them take formal classes and practice hard, too. Still, only a handful will ever achieve the kind of success Carolyn has.

It would be easy to say that she is lucky or that she has exceptional natural talent. The truth is that yes, Carolyn is gifted, but she also works incredibly hard. She is humble, sweet and unassuming. In addition, Carolyn is highly respected by other dancers because of the great obstacles she's overcome to become one of the greatest dancers in the world.

The sacrifices she has made are truly amazing. While other kids are at the mall, Carolyn is doing painful back exercises. While friends are watching television and playing video games, Carolyn is taking endless dance classes, perfecting her technique. While her classmates have fun together at school, Carolyn sits alone at her computer, trying to get all her work done in a short amount of time so that she can squeeze in a few extra hours to train.

Her typical day is filled from the moment she wakes up until long after most kids have gone to sleep. Most days begin with an early visit to the chiropractor's office. A chiropractor is a doctor who is trained to work on the alignment of the spine. For Carolyn, this means "adjusting" her back to make sure that the vertebrae are aligned, minimizing the daily pain she feels.

After seeing her chiropractor, Carolyn does traction, which pulls her body to relieve pressure on the spine. Then she is ready for her Wobble Chair exercises. These are specific exercises that are designed to increase her balance and to strengthen the muscles in her lower back. They look funny, but can be very difficult and painful if you have scoliosis.

Most dancers spend the majority of their time practicing dance. For Carolyn, she must *double* that amount of time. Prior to dancing for even one minute, she has to perform hours of grueling therapy for her scoliosis… just to get her body to a place where she *can* dance.

Her afternoon therapy consists of two hours of strengthening exercises. These exercises are for all areas of her body. They include lower back raises, weight training for upper body strength, abdominal exercises, the stationary bike for endurance, and leg exercises to prepare her body for the many jumps she must do in her routines. After two hours of exercising, Carolyn is ready to actually dance! She can only dance for one hour, though. That's because when the sun goes down, Carolyn has to finish her schoolwork and eat dinner. After that, she heads down to the dance studio for her formal training.

Each evening Carolyn practices a different dance style. On Mondays, she takes lyrical dance lessons for an hour, followed by 90 minutes of modern dance. On Tuesdays, it's two hours of ballet and one hour as a teacher's assistant in a modern dance class. Wednesdays mean two more hours of ballet. She has one hour of tap and one 90-minute jazz session on Thursdays. Her classes last until 9:00 at night, every night, except Friday. On Fridays she gets a night of rest, so that she is ready to head back on Saturdays for group rehearsals. Sounds grueling, doesn't it?

Carolyn's training schedule is incredibly full, leaving little time for family and friends. Like most competitive dancers, her social circle revolves around her dance life.  Her friends are dancers who understand the dedication it takes to maintain this lifestyle. They understand that Carolyn must watch her diet closely, sleep well, not risk injury and keep her focus solely on dance. They can also appreciate the physical hardships that go along with competitive dancing.

For dancers, the pain and suffering begins with their feet. Carolyn's feet are permanently scarred from the drawstrings that hold her slippers on. The strings must be pulled extremely tight, which leaves dark spots on her skin. In addition to the spots, her feet are always covered with blisters and calluses, while her toenails are constantly black and blue. Carolyn says she can't even count the number of toenails she has lost!

	Physical pain and a demanding lifestyle are the price of success as a competitive dancer. Carolyn competes in seven major competitions each year, so her tight schedule is maintained year-round. Every title that Carolyn wins is the culmination of grueling hours of dance training and physical therapy. These hours take their toll on her body—a body ravaged daily by scoliosis.
	Carolyn has marched on despite her worsening spinal curve. She won't let scoliosis keep her from achieving her goals, and she certainly wouldn't let it stop her from dancing in Germany at the World Championships.

# Chapter Eight

## World Championships

    Carolyn watched the clouds fall away as she thought about what lay ahead. This was the trip she had been preparing for all year: the International Dance Organization World Championships, the Olympics of dance. Like all great athletes, she had paid her dues for the chance to represent her country. That's what this was all about. Like Olympians, dancers don't receive monetary rewards, only the recognition of their incredible talent and the honor of representing their country. That was more than enough for Carolyn.

    Accompanying Carolyn to Germany was her mother, Miss Andrea and other dancers from the United States. Several of the girls on the dance team were friends of Carolyn's, so she knew the trip was going to be a lot of fun. Dancers are a close-knit group, despite often competing against one another.

Traveling to Europe to compete definitely added to the excitement. Still, competitions are very intense and time-consuming, so there isn't much time for sightseeing. Carolyn competed in Daytona Beach, Florida, five times and never even stepped on the beach there. Germany would probably be no different.

Prior to stepping onto the airplane, Carolyn researched things that she might see and do in Germany, despite her limited time there. She learned key phrases and mentally prepared herself to eat German food, which would be a complete change from her strict diet. She was excited to immerse herself in a different culture, even if it was only for a few days.

You can imagine Carolyn's reaction when she stepped outside the airport in Dresden, Germany, and the first thing she saw was a McDonald's. Unfortunately for Carolyn, the rest of her German cultural experience was about the same. When they finally got to their hotel in Riesa, Germany, after 12 hours of flying, they decided to eat in the hotel restaurant so they could get right to bed afterward. Carolyn was excited for her first taste of German food, only to be disappointed again. The two restaurants in the hotel served American food.

The next day they had some time in the early afternoon and went out in search of real German cuisine. They found a small restaurant owned by an Iraqi man, thinking that at least it would be different, but all he served was Italian food.

Sightseeing adventures were also very limited. Riesa is a very small industrial town in eastern Germany, and there really isn't much to see. When the Erdgas Sports Arena opened in 2004, Riesa became a sports town. The arena is the largest multipurpose event center in eastern Germany, and it dominates the small town. Guarded by large statues of sumo wrestlers, this arena was a daunting sight for Carolyn. She had never performed in such a large venue and felt a bit overwhelmed by it.

**The Erdgas Sports Arena in Riesa.**

When Carolyn awoke on opening day, she was excited and nervous. People were fascinated by the dancers from the United States, constantly stopping them to take pictures. Simply trying to get to breakfast was difficult because the cameras were everywhere. Carolyn received even more attention than the other girls. Local people stopped and stared at her wherever she went. At first she thought it was because of her back brace, so she didn't worry too much about it. Soon she discovered that it wasn't that at all: It turned out that many of these people had rarely, if ever, seen an African-American girl. At first their fascination was amusing, but Carolyn tired of it very quickly.

The start of the World Championship competition made Carolyn quickly forget the stares. The competition is set up in rounds—each round taking place in front of a capacity crowd. All of the 92 dancers in Carolyn's Senior Solo category would dance in the first round. The judges would eliminate half of the dancers after that one dance. So, round two would begin with just 46 dancers remaining. Each round after that would eliminate half of the dancers, until they were down to the final six.

There was a ton of pressure involved in this event. Each time someone danced, it was a stand-alone performance, which meant that none of her previous dances counted. If a dancer made a mistake in any round, she would be eliminated. In addition to that, international judges can be very different than U.S. judges, so it's hard to know how a performance will be received.

Carolyn chose to dance to "Blackbird," which was the dance that had gotten her into the competition. Her confidence in this dance definitely came through in her movements. Carolyn is only 5'1" tall, but when she performs she seems larger than life, dominating the stage. The judges obviously saw her great talent, because she easily made it through the first three rounds.

By the final round the pressure was intense and the competition fierce. All the dancers were exceptional—the best of the best from around the world. Carolyn knew that to stand out she would have to increase the technical difficulty of her dance, so she added the penchée, an extremely tricky move, to her routine for the final round. During the penchée, the dancer is balanced on one knee with the other leg straight out to the side. The arms are also out to the sides. While balanced in this position, the dancer must keep her shoulders in line over her hips, then dip her torso down and back up without letting the position of her legs or arms change.

If that weren't enough, Carolyn made the move even harder. While in the original position on one knee, Carolyn slightly lifted the foot on her bent leg and turned her entire body. Instead of facing front, she was now facing stage right. Carolyn had worked on this move in practice, but had never gotten it just right. It was now or never…

Amazingly, she did it—gracefully executing the difficult move as if she had been doing it forever. She had taken a big risk and come through. Unfortunately, it still was not enough to win the competition. Carolyn had danced her best, though, so when they announced her name for fourth place, she wasn't at all disappointed. After all, this wasn't fourth place at some regional competition—this was fourth place in the *world*!

Carolyn didn't think there was any way to top that, but the closing ceremony came close. There was a parade of flags, just like in the Olympics. Carolyn and her teammates, dressed in red, white and blue sweat suits with their names printed on the back, proudly carried the American flag as they paraded into the massive arena. There were dancers representing over 30 different countries. Carolyn was thrilled to be with all these talented dancers. She stood in awe, listening to the loud cheers that shook the stands.

*Where do I go from here?* Carolyn asked herself on the plane ride home to the States. Since she was eight, her entire world has revolved around dance. Now Carolyn must decide what she will do with her future, and how big a role dance will play. She definitely has a ton of options. Many dancers in Florida, where Carolyn lives, go on to perform on cruise ships, since that is the big entertainment industry there. But Carolyn has no desire to do that. She could always follow the path of other dancers before her, like Madonna, and head to New York City to audition for a dance company. But because of her scoliosis and all the care it requires, living alone in New York doesn't seem likely right now either.

Carolyn is a gifted athlete who has sacrificed a lot to dance. Still, she knows that because of her health issues, she must be realistic about her options. Dancing, like other professional sports, is extremely hard on the body. A dance career is usually very short, often less than 10 years—and that's if you have perfect health. Carolyn's professional dance career may be much shorter than that. She recognizes that there is always the possibility that back surgery will become necessary, preventing her from continuing to dance in the future.

For now, though, Carolyn is not ready to give up dance. Her immediate plans are to attend college to study dance and English literature. She made the decision to attend a school close to home so she can continue physical therapy. Beyond that, she is considering a career as a dance instructor, which will give her an opportunity to share the experience she has gained.

Of course, Carolyn hopes that someday soon she will be able to return to Haiti to visit her family. She hopes that Haiti will find peace and stability—reinventing itself as the beautiful, wondrous homeland she experienced during her childhood.

**These are the flowers which line the front yard of Carolyn's grandparents house in Port-au-Prince. They often come to her mind when she thinks Haiti.**

First, Carolyn has one more major dance competition. This summer, she will be heading to New York with the hope of becoming Miss Dance of America. This would truly be the crowning moment of her dance life. Prior to going to Germany, Carolyn placed first in the Miss Dance of Florida competition, earning her the right to compete for the title of Miss Dance of America.

This competition is unique because it involves more than just dancing; it is designed to find the most well-rounded dancer. Dancers are judged on one dance performance, an interview, a written essay and audition classes, where the dancers are observed learning new dance steps.

In her essay for the competition, Carolyn states, "Dance is more than just movement; it is a companion. Dance has not only taught me how to effectively express my emotions, but it has become a means by which to search within myself to find what lies beneath the exaggerated movements. Dance has shown me the universal sufferings and joys all people endure and how to appeal to the qualities that connect us as people. Like a good friend, it has also revealed to me my own strengths and weaknesses and how to persevere through uncertainty. I have learned to love myself, not because of any perceived greatness, but because I am a unique individual."

Carolyn is definitely unique *and* talented. This will be her last competition with her dance company, and to actually be crowned Miss Dance of America would be the ultimate recognition of her incredible talent. Even more than that, it would mean that Carolyn is not just a phenomenal dancer, but that she embodies all of the characteristics that make dance such a beautiful art form.

Regardless of the outcome, Carolyn has proven that she has the heart of a champion. Loren Foster, the choreographer who worked with Carolyn on her dance for "Blackbird," described Carolyn to the local paper like this: "Carolyn is a dream to choreograph because she can do any movement you dream up and bring it to life. She makes something impossible, possible."

That statement is true of Carolyn both on and off the dance

floor. She makes the impossible, possible—like defying the odds by dancing in spite of her scoliosis. For 12 years, she has exhibited amazing passion, fighting twice as hard as her competitors. This drive to succeed has helped her rise to the top of one of the most competitive sports in America. Carolyn's passion for dance took her from being an uncoordinated child with a serious deformity to being one of the most graceful, talented dancers in the world. It's that passion that will keep her dancing long after the stage lights fade.